Lara /.

Table of Contents

Introduction:

Hi my name is Lara. I am a 10 year old girl and I love to bake.

I have been baking even more during lockdown. I have put together some of my favourite recipes that I have been making during this time. There are a mixture of cookies, cakes, drinks and more in this book all of which my family and I love to eat.

Half of any money I make from selling this cookbook will go to Naomi House and Jack's Place, children's hospices (www.naomihouse.org.uk) because I want to help children who are ill.

Here is a picture of me baking with my dog Ellie!

APPLE CRUMBLE
– very easy and very yummy!

Ingredients:

- ➤ Oats 1 tablespoon
- ➤ Butter 110g
- ➤ Apples 575g
- ➤ Water
- ➤ Plain Flour 175g
- ➤ Brown sugar 110g
- ➤ Demerara sugar 1 tablespoon

Tools that you need:

- ➤ Mixing bowl
- ➤ Tablespoon measure
- ➤ Weighing scales
- ➤ Saucepan
- ➤ Peeling Knife
- ➤ Wooden Spoon
- ➤ Oven proof dish

What you need to do:

➤ First heat the oven to 190 degrees centigrade (375 degrees Fahrenheit).

➤ Then peel, core and chop your apples into chunks your apples. Now put your apples into your saucepan with 2 tablespoons of water and cook on a low heat until the apples are a little soft. Take the apples out and put in your ovenproof dish and flatten down with the back of the wooden spoon.

➤ Now put your flour and brown sugar in your mixing bowl. Slice in your butter and rub it in with your fingertips until the mixture looks like breadcrumbs. Pour the breadcrumb mix over the apples to form a pile in the centre then use your wooden spoon to even out. Sprinkle 1 tablespoon of oats and 1 tablespoon of demerara sugar over evenly.

➤ Set on baking tray and put the preheated oven for 35-40 minutes, until the top is golden and the apples feel very soft when you insert a small knife through the crumble. Leave to cool for 10 minutes before serving. Now you have a yummy crumble!

TIP: If you want to you can add in other fruits to your apple mix, like blueberries, blackberries or raspberries to mix it up!

APPLE PIE
– in case you don't like crumble!

Ingredients:

- Ready made shortcrust pastry
- 5 medium sized Apples or more if you have a big pie tin
- Water
- 2 tablespoons Caster Sugar
- Flour for dusting

Tools that you need:

- Rolling pin
- Chopping Board
- Pie tin
- Wooden Spoon
- Saucepan
- Peeling knife
- Tablespoon measure

What you need to do:

- First you preheat your oven to 160 degrees centigrade or 320 degrees Fahrenheit.

➢ Then peel, core and chop the apples place into the saucepan. Add two tablespoons of water and caster sugar. Place onto low to medium heat and constantly stir until soft. Then take off heat.

➢ Rollout your pastry, you may need to use some flour to dust your rolling surface so the pastry doesn't stick, and cut it to fit your pie tin. Grease your pie tin. Place your pastry into your tin remove the apples from the saucepan with a wooden spoon and place them onto the pastry in the tin. Cut out a pastry lid to fit the tin then place on and prick the pastry with a fork.

➢ Then place in the oven for 20-30 minutes or until cooked and golden and tasting lovely.

Lara Ramsay

BANANA CAKE
a little bit healthy as it has fruit in it!

Ingredients:

- Plain Flour 175g
- Baking powder 1 teaspoon
- Bicarbonate of soda ½ teaspoon
- Butter 125g
- Sugar 150g
- Eggs 2 large or 3 small
- Banana 3 or 300g
- Vanilla extract 1 teaspoon

Tools that you need:

- 3 bowls
- 1 teaspoon measure
- Scales
- A loaf tin
- Banana masher or large fork
- Wooden spoon
- Electric mixer
- A baking tin liner

- ½ teaspoon measure
- Cooling rack

What you need to do:

- First you turn the oven to 175 degrease centigrade or 350 degrees Fahrenheit.

- Then you get your first bowl and measure your flour then add it into the bowl. Then add your baking powder and bicarbonate of soda and mix it with a wooden spoon. Then set that bowl aside and grab your other bowl and add your butter and sugar. Then mix these together with your electric mixer then one at time while mixing add the eggs to the butter and sugar mixture.

- Once this is finished in the third bowl mash your bananas with the banana masher. Then add the mashed bananas to the butter sugar and egg mixture. Then add in the vanilla extract and mix with the wooden spoon.

- Then add the flour mixture to the main banana mixture. Then put the baking liner in the baking tin and then add your mixture to the tin and bake for 45 minutes.

TIP: You can add chocolate chips to this mixture too!

BLUEBERRY MUFFINS
– more fruit!

Ingredients:

- ➢ Butter 100g
- ➢ Caster sugar 140g
- ➢ Large eggs 2
- ➢ Natural yogurt 140g
- ➢ Vanilla extract 1 teaspoon
- ➢ Milk 2 tablespoons
- ➢ Plain Flour 250g
- ➢ Baking powder 2 teaspoons
- ➢ Bicarbonate of soda 1 teaspoon
- ➢ Blueberries 125g

Tools that you need:

- ➢ Muffin Tin
- ➢ Paper cases
- ➢ Electric mixer
- ➢ 2 Mixing bowls
- ➢ Spoon measures
- ➢ Wooden spoon

➢ Cooling rack
➢ Scales

What you need to do:

➢ First heat the oven to 200 degrees centigrade or 390 degrees Fahrenheit and line a 12 hole Muffin tin with your paper cases.

➢ Put your butter and caster sugar in a mixing bowl and then beat the butter and caster sugar together using an electric mixer until it is pale and fluffy. Add in your eggs and beat with the electric mixer for about 1 min. Then mix in the yoghurt, vanilla extract and milk using a wooden spoon.

➢ Put your flour, baking powder and bicarbonate of soda in your second mixing bowl and mix with your wooden spoon. Then tip this into the first bowl and stir in using your wooden spoon.

➢ Then mix in the blueberries gently with your wooden spoon. Put this mixture in the muffin cases. Bake for 5 mins, then reduce the oven to 180 degrees centigrade (360 degrees Fahrenheit|), I set the oven timer to go off to remind me when to turn the oven down. Bake for 15-18 mins more until the muffins have risen and golden. Put a cocktail stick into the centre and if they are ready it will come out clean.

➢ Cool in the tin for 10 mins, then carefully lift out onto a wire rack to finish cooling.

1 lb = 12.5g

BROWNIES
– just yummy!

Ingredients:

- ➤ Butter 250g
- ➤ Cocoa powder 1 tablespoon
- ➤ Sugar 1 ½ cups
- ➤ Eggs 4
- ➤ Flour 1 cup
- ➤ Baking powder 1 teaspoon
- ➤ Vanilla extract 1 teaspoon

Tools that you need:

- ➤ Mixing bowl
- ➤ Scales
- ➤ Tablespoon measure
- ➤ Cup measurer
- ➤ Teaspoon measure
- ➤ Wooden spoon
- ➤ Baking tray
- ➤ Baking tray liner
- ➤ Cooling rack

➢ Electric mixer

What you need to do:

➢ First you turn the oven to 180 degrees centigrade (360 degrees Fahrenheit).

➢ Then you get your mixing bowl and put your butter and sugar in the bowl and then mix with your electric mixer. Then start adding in your eggs one at a time and mix again with your electric mixer. Next add in your vanilla extract and mix again.

➢ Then add in your flour and baking powder and stir for 1 min with your wooden spoon. Then add your cocoa powder and mix with the wooden spoon

➢ Then put your mixture into the lined baking tray and put in the oven for 45 mins. Then take it out and let it cool for 5 mins on a cooling rack before taking out of tin and then you will have the best brownies ever!

CARROT CAKE
– more healthy as it has vegetables in it!

Ingredients:

- ➢ Muscovado sugar 175g
- ➢ Sunflower oil 175ml
- ➢ Large eggs lightly beaten 3
- ➢ Grated carrot 140g
- ➢ Raisins 100g
- ➢ Grated zest of orange 1
- ➢ Self-raising flour 175g
- ➢ Bicarbonate of soda 1 teaspoon
- ➢ Ground cinnamon 1 teaspoon
- ➢ Grated nutmeg ½ teaspoon

Tools that you need:

- ➢ Square cake tin
- ➢ Baking parchment paper
- ➢ 2 Mixing bowls
- ➢ Wooden spoon
- ➢ Grater
- ➢ Sieve

- ➤ Cooling rack
- ➤ Electric mixer
- ➤ Spoon measures

What you need to do:

- ➤ First preheat the oven to 180 degrees centigrade (360 degrees Fahrenheit). Oil and line the base and the sides of a square cake tin with baking parchment.

- ➤ Put your eggs in your first bowl and beat together with your electric mixer or a large fork. Then tip your muscovado sugar, sunflower oil and the beaten eggs into your second larger mixing bowl. Lightly mix them with a wooden spoon. Then mix in your grated carrots, raisins and grated zest from the orange with a wooden spoon.

- ➤ Sieve the self-raising flour, bicarbonate of soda, ground cinnamon and grated nutmeg into this bowl. Mix everything together with your wooden spoon. Your mixture will be soft and almost runny. Pour this mixture into your baking tin and bake for 40-45 mins or until it feels firm and springy when you press gently in the centre. If you put a cocktail stick in the centre it should come out clean.

- ➤ Cool in the tin for 5 mins, then turn it out, peel off the paper and cool on a wire rack.

CHOCOLATE CAKE
– great with icing!

Ingredients:

- Flour 200g
- Baking powder 1 teaspoon
- Bicarbonate of soda 1 teaspoon
- Butter 200g
- Sugar 200g
- 5 Eggs
- Cocoa powder 2 tablespoons

Tools that you need:

- 2 mixing bowls
- Teaspoon measure
- Scales
- Wooden spoon
- 1 tablespoon measure
- Loaf tin
- Baking liner
- Electric mixer
- Cooling rack

What you need to do:

➢ First you turn the oven to 175 degrees centigrade (350 degrees Fahrenheit). Then grab your mixing bowl and add your flour. then add your baking powder and bicarbonate of soda and mix with your wooden spoon.

➢ Then grab your second bowl and beat together your butter and sugar with your electric mixer. Then one at a time add in your eggs. Then beat in with the electric mixer. Next start adding in cocoa powder and stir in with your wooden spoon.

➢ Then get your first bowl with the flour mixture and slowly add this into your second bowl folding in the mixture with your wooden spoon. Then put your baking tin liner in your loaf tin. Then put all your mixture in the loaf tin. Now put the loaf tin in the oven and bake for 45 minutes.

➢ Once it is cooked then you should put it on a wire rack to cool. Then you'll have the greatest cake ever!

CHOCOLATE CHIP COOKIES
– best ever!

Ingredients:

- ➤ Butter 150g
- ➤ Light Brown sugar ½ cup
- ➤ Sugar ½ cup
- ➤ 1 Egg
- ➤ Flour 1 ¾ cup
- ➤ Chocolate chips, however many you want

Tools that you need:

- ➤ A mixing bowl
- ➤ ½ cup measurer
- ➤ 1 cup measurer
- ➤ ¾ cup measurer
- ➤ Scales
- ➤ Baking tray
- ➤ Baking tray liner
- ➤ Wooden spoon
- ➤ Electric mixer
- ➤ Cooling rack

What you need to do:

➤ First you turn your oven to 180 degrees centigrade (360 degrees Fahrenheit).

➤ Then you get your mixing bowl and add your butter and the light brown sugar then mix together with an electric mixer. Then add your caster sugar and the egg. Then mix again. Then slowly add in your flour and slowly mix it in with your wooden spoon.

➤ Then you can add in your chocolate chips. Now you can shape your mixture into round balls and put on the baking tray. Then put the tray in the oven for 10 mins.

➤ Then, when you take them out to cool, you'll have the most wonderful chocolate chip cookies!

CHOCOLATE CHIP SHORTBREAD
– great to dip in a glass of milk!

Ingredients:

- ➢ 300g Plain Flour
- ➢ 200g butter
- ➢ 1 egg yolk
- ➢ 100g caster sugar
- ➢ 80g milk choc chips

Tools that you will need:

- ➢ Large mixing bowl
- ➢ Sieve
- ➢ Wooden spoon
- ➢ Baking Tray
- ➢ Baking Liner
- ➢ Cling film
- ➢ Rolling pin
- ➢ Baking Parchment
- ➢ Sharp knife
- ➢ Spatula
- ➢ Cooling rack

What you will need to do:

> ➤ Turn on the oven to 170 degrees centigrade (340 degrees Fahrenheit)

> ➤ Then you need to sieve the flour into the large mixing bowl and then add the butter and rub it into the flour with your fingertips, until it is like crumbs. Then you stir through the egg yolk, sugar and choc chips. Mix it with your wooden spoon. Then squish it into a ball of dough. Wrap in cling film and put int in the fridge for 30 mins.

> ➤ Take it out of the fridge. Roll out the dough with your rolling pin between two sheets of baking parchment paper. Roll until its about 1cm thick. Take the top sheet of parchment paper off and cut it into squares with a sharp knife. Put these squares onto your lined baking sheet with your spatula. Leave space between them as they spread in the oven.

> ➤ Put in oven for 15-20mins or until lightly golden. Take out of the oven and allow to cool for 10 mins before putting them on the cooling rack.

CHOCOLATE RICE CRISPIE CAKES
– very easy!

Ingredients:

➢ Milk Chocolate 150g
➢ Rice crispy 120g
➢ Butter 100g

Tools that you will need:

➢ Saucepan
➢ Cupcake Tray
➢ Cupcake cases
➢ Wooden spoon

What you need to do:

➢ First you place your saucepan on a low heat and start melting your butter and once the butter is melted you can add your chocolate into your melted butter and melt as well. Then when you have melted your butter you can take off the heat and add in your rice crispies.

➢ Then put in your cupcake cases and put the tray to cool in the fridge then once they have hardened they are ready to eat and will be very yummy

COOKIES
– plain and easy but super tasty!

Ingredients:

➢ 125g soft butter
➢ 100g light brown sugar
➢ 125g caster sugar
➢ 1 egg
➢ 1 teaspoon vanilla extract
➢ 225g self raising flour

Tools that you will need:

➢ Bowl
➢ Scales
➢ Teaspoon measurer
➢ Baking tray
➢ Baking tray liner
➢ Wooden spoon
➢ Cooling Rack

What you need to do:

➢ First you turn the oven to 180 degrees centigrade (350 degrees Fahrenheit)

➤ Then you get your bowl and add your soft butter and light brown sugar and mix together with your wooden spoon. Then add your caster sugar and eggs and mix together again with the wooden spoon. Then add your vanilla extract and mix. Then slowly add in your flour and mix together.

➤ You should now have a dough like mixture. Take lumps from this dough mixture and squish them using your hands into round shapes on your lined baking tray. You will need to leave spaces between your dough shapes as they will spread in the oven!

➤ Then put your tray in the oven for 8-10 mins until the cookies are going brown and you when you take them out you will have the most delicious cookies!

DOUGHNUTS
– super yummy but take a little longer

Ingredients:

- 240ml Milk
- 50g caster sugar plus 1 teaspoon
- 2 ¼ teaspoon dried yeast
- 500g Plain flour
- ½ teaspoon salt
- 6 tablespoons melted butter
- 2 large eggs
- ½ teaspoon vanilla extract
- Vegetable oil
- Sprinkles, if you want

For glaze:

- 60ml water
- 250g icing sugar
- ½ teaspoon vanilla extract

Tools you will need:

- Small Bowl

➢ Spoon

➢ 2 Medium Bowls

➢ 2 Large bowls

➢ Electric mixer

➢ Tea towel

➢ Baking Tray

➢ Baking Parchment

➢ Saucepan

➢ Slotted Spoon

➢ Plate

➢ Kitchen Towel

What you need to do:

➢ Microwave your milk in a small bowl for 40 seconds. Then add a teaspoon of sugar and stir until it has all mixed in. Then sprinkle over your yeast and let it sit there until it gets all bubbly after about 8 minutes.

➢ Get your medium bowl and stir together your flour and salt. In your large bowl add your sugar, butter, eggs and vanilla extract and mix together with your electric mixer. Then pour in the sugar and yeast mixture from your small bowl and mix with a wooden spoon.

➢ Then add in the flour and salt from your second bowl and stir together with your spoon until you get a messy dough like mixture. Put this dough onto a surface which has some flour on it and knead it until it gets all stretchy and not so sticky. Then put this ball of dough into another large bowl that has been oiled and cover with a clean tea towel. Leave this in a warm place for about an hour and it will have doubled in size!

> Punch the air out of the dough – this is great fun! And roll out the dough on your baking parchment and either use different sized cookie cutters to make ring doughnuts or make doughnut balls and doughnut rings using your hands. Cover these doughnut rings and balls with a tea towel to rise again.

> Then take your saucepan and put in your vegetable oil and put it over a medium-high heat. The first time I did this my Mum did it with me as oil can get very hot and burn you! So be careful and ask a grown up to help.

> Once the oil is hot put in your doughnuts and they will float to the top of the oil when they start cooking and will need 1-2 minutes each side to become all golden and cooked. Then take them out carefully and put on a plate with kitchen towel on it. Once they are all cooked and cooling you can make your glaze.

> Mix together your icing sugar, water and vanilla essence together in a medium bowl. Once the doughnuts are cooled dip into the glaze and add sprinkles if you want. Then you have the best doughnuts ever!

ETON MESS
– less cooking, just more mixing!

Ingredients:

> ➢ 2 small pots Double Cream
> ➢ Meringues (shop bought is ok)
> ➢ Raspberries

Tools that you need:

> ➢ Mixing bowl
> ➢ Electric mixer
> ➢ Serving bowl
> ➢ Wooden spoon

What you need to do:

> ➢ First you pour your double cream into your mixing bowl. Mix with your electric mixer until thick. Break up the meringues and put a layer of these broken meringues into your serving bowl. Spoon layer of double cream on top of the meringues. Add a layer of raspberries on top. Do this two more times for all 3 layers and you will have the best Eton mess ever!

ICE CREAM
– you do need an ice cream maker!

Ingredients:

> ➢ 2 cups Double Cream
> ➢ 1 cup Whole milk
> ➢ 1 cup caster sugar
> ➢ Flavouring – any, whatever you want

Tools that you need:

> ➢ Cup measure
> ➢ Ice cream maker
> ➢ Spoon

What you need to do:

> ➢ First add your cream to your ice cream maker pot. Then add your milk to your cream and then mix together with your wooden spoon. Then add your sugar and flavouring to the mixture.

> ➢ Then put it in your ice cream maker for one hour and then you will have the greatest ice cream ever!

Lara Ramsay

46

LEMONADE
– nice, refreshing drink

Ingredients:

- ➢ 4 unwaxed lemons
- ➢ 140g caster sugar
- ➢ 1 litre cold water
- ➢ Ice cubes

Tools that you will need:

- ➢ Jug
- ➢ Scales
- ➢ Measuring jug
- ➢ Lemon squeezer
- ➢ Spoon
- ➢ Bowl

What you need to do:

- ➢ Add your cold water into your jug. Measure out the sugar and pour it all into the water and stir it until the sugar has dissolved.
- ➢ Then squeeze the lemon juice out of the lemons using your squeezer. Then pour all the lemon juice into the jug and

stir. Add ice cubes into the jug and then you are done!

LEMON CAKE
– when my Mum has garden visitors this is always one of their favourites!

Ingredients

- ➤ 200g Self Raising Flour
- ➤ 200g Butter
- ➤ 200g Sugar
- ➤ 5 Eggs
- ➤ Lemon juice from a real ½ lemon

Tools you will need:

- ➤ Mixing bowl
- ➤ Weighing scales
- ➤ Wooden Spoon
- ➤ Baking Tin
- ➤ Baking Tin Liner
- ➤ Electric Mixer

What you need to do:

- ➤ First you turn the oven to 175 degrees centigrade (350 degrees Fahrenheit).
- ➤ Then you put your butter and sugar in the bowl then mix

them together with your electric mixer. Then slowly add your eggs one at a time and mix after adding each egg. Then add in your lemon juice and mix in gradually with your wooden spoon. Add in your flour and mix gradually with your wooden spoon. Then add your mixture into your baking tin. Then put it in the oven for 45 mins.

➢ Then you'll have the best lemon cake!

TIP: Add butter icing with some lemon zest or lemon juice on top of the cake for extra lemon!

LAYER CAKE
– this looks cool!

Ingredients:

- ➤ 200g Plain Flour
- ➤ 1 teaspoon Baking Powder
- ➤ 1 teaspoon Bicarbonate of soda
- ➤ 200g butter
- ➤ 200g caster sugar
- ➤ 5 eggs
- ➤ 3 teaspoon vanilla extract
- ➤ Food colouring – you choose what colours you like!

Tools you will need:

- ➤ 2 mixing bowls
- ➤ 1 teaspoon measure
- ➤ Wooden spoon
- ➤ 2 x Layer baking tins
- ➤ Electric mixer
- ➤ Cooling racks
- ➤ **Scales**

What you should do:

> ➢ First you should turn the oven on to 175 degrees centigrade (350 degrees Fahrenheit).

> ➢ Then you get your first mixing bowl and add your flour. Then you add your baking powder and bicarbonate of soda to that bowl and mix.

> ➢ Then you get your second mixing bowl and add your butter and sugar and mix with your electric mixer. Then you slowly add your eggs one at a time and mixing with the electric mixer after you have added each one. Then you add the vanilla extract and stir in

> ➢ Then you get your first bowl that had your flour mixture in it and then add it to your butter/sugar/egg mixture slowly and mix carefully with your wooden spoon.

> ➢ Then split your mixture equally between the two bowls and add a different colour to each one – whatever colour you like! Then put the mixture into the two baking tins and put them in the oven for 35 mins.

> ➢ Once they are cooked take them out of the oven and put them on the cooling racks whilst you make the butter icing to go in the middle of the two layers once they have cooled. Then you'll have the best cake ever!

MARBLE CAKE
– all swirly!

Ingredients:

- ➢ 200g plain flour
- ➢ 1 teaspoon Baking Powder
- ➢ 1 teaspoon Bicarbonate of soda
- ➢ 200g caster sugar
- ➢ 200g butter
- ➢ 4 eggs
- ➢ 2 teaspoon vanilla extract
- ➢ 1 tablespoon of cocoa powder

Tools you will need:

- ➢ 3 mixing bowls
- ➢ Weighing scales
- ➢ Baking tin liner
- ➢ Baking tin
- ➢ 1 teaspoon measurer
- ➢ 1 tablespoon measurer
- ➢ Wooden spoon
- ➢ Metal spoon

- ➢ Baking tin
- ➢ Electric mixer
- ➢ Cooling rack

What you need to do:

- ➢ First turn the oven on to 175 degrees centigrade (350 degrees Fahrenheit).
- ➢ Then get one mixing bowl and put your flour in and also your baking powder and bicarbonate of soda and mix together with a wooden spoon.
- ➢ Then get the second mixing bowl and add your butter and sugar and beat together with the electric mixer. Then add your eggs one at a time and beat them in with the electric mixer. Then slowly fold in the flour mixture from the first bowl into your second bowl using the wooden spoon.
- ➢ Take half this mixture and put it in a third mixing bowl. Take the vanilla essence and gently stir it into one of the two mixtures. Then stir the cocoa powder into the mixture in the third mixing bowl and mix carefully and completely.
- ➢ Put the baking tin liner into the baking tin and pour in all the vanilla mixture into the tin. Then pour the chocolate mixture on top of the vanilla mixture and swirl together gently with a metal spoon.
- ➢ Then put the baking tin in the oven for 45 minutes and you'll have the best marble cake ever!

MARSHMALLOW RICE CRISPIE CAKES
– very easy but very sticky!

Ingredients:

- ➤ Marshmallows
- ➤ Rice crispies
- ➤ Butter

Tools that you will need:

- ➤ Saucepan
- ➤ Wooden spoon
- ➤ Baking Tray

What you need to do:

- ➤ First you put your butter in the saucepan over a low heat and wait until it has melted. Then add in your marshmallows and stir them into the butter until the marshmallows melt as well. Use the wooden spoon to mix the butter and marshmallows together.

- ➤ Then take the mixture off the heat and add in your rice crispies and mix together with your wooden spoon. Then spoon the mixture into your baking tray and cool in the fridge and you'll have the most delicious food ever.

MILKSHAKES
– can be healthy or not!

Ingredients:

- ➤ 1/3 cup of milk
- ➤ 1 ½ cups of vanilla ice cream
- ➤ Flavour – any that you like
- ➤ Toppings – however much you want

Tools that you need:

- ➤ Blender or smoothie mixer
- ➤ 1/3 cup measurer
- ➤ ½ cup measurer

What you need to do:

- ➤ First you add your milk and your ice cream to the blender or smoothie maker. You then also add whatever flavourings you would like eg. Chocolate syrup, strawberries. Then you blend this mixture.
- ➤ Once you have poured this mixture into a glass you can add whatever toppings you would like and make the best milkshake ever!

MILLIONAIRE'S SHORTBREAD
– or Millionation Bread according to my cousin Eliza!

Ingredients:

- 250g Plain Flour
- 75g caster sugar
- 225g butter
- 50g light muscovado sugar
- 397g can of condensed milk
- 150g milk chocolate

Tools that you will need:

- 2 bowls
- Scales
- Swiss roll tin
- Fork
- 2 x Saucepan
- Spatula
- Scales
- Wooden spoon

What you need to do:

➤ Turn the oven on to 180 degrees centigrade (360 degrees Fahrenheit) and lightly grease with butter a 30 cm X 20cm rectangular tin which is at least 3cm deep.

➤ To make the shortbread, mix the plain flour and caster sugar in one mixing bowl. Rub in the butter until it makes a dough. Then press the dough into the prepared baking tin. Bake it in the oven for 20 mins until it is light golden. Then take it out of the over and place it to one side.

➤ To make the caramel, put the butter, light muscovado sugar and condensed milk into a saucepan. Put the pan on a medium heat and stir until the butter has melted and the sugar has dissolved. Then turn down to a low heat and stir constantly for about 5-10 mins or until the mixture has thickened. Pour this over the shortbread and put the tin into the fridge for about 1 hour.

➤ For the chocolate, fill a saucepan with water. Put your chocolate in a ceramic bowl and put it in the saucepan. Heat the water in the saucepan on a medium heat and wait for the chocolate to melt. Then use your spatula to pour the melted chocolate over the cold caramel and then put the tin back in the fridge for about 30 mins until the chocolate has set.

NUTELLA FUDGE CAKE
– only 3 ingredients needed!

Ingredients:

- ➤ 4 eggs
- ➤ 750g Nutella
- ➤ 1 1/3 cups of plain flour

Tools that you will need:

- ➤ Round cake tin
- ➤ Scales
- ➤ Cup measure
- ➤ Baking liner
- ➤ Mixing bowl
- ➤ Wooden spoon
- ➤ Electric mixer
- ➤ Sieve

What you need to do:

- ➤ First turn the oven on to 160 degrees centigrade.
- ➤ Put all your eggs into the mixing bowl and add 2 cups of Nutella and beat with the electric mixer for about 5

minutes until it is all smooth.

➢ Sieve the flour into the bowl and fold the flour using your wooden spoon into the Nutella and egg mixture.

➢ Line your baking tin with the baking liner and then pour your mixture into the tin and put it in the oven for about 45 minutes.

➢ Once the cake has cooled you can spread the Nutella that is left over the top

OAT BISCUITS
– for my Scottish Dad!

Ingredients:

- ➤ 160g soft butter
- ➤ 0.6 cup caster sugar
- ➤ 3 tablespoons golden syrup
- ➤ 1 cup Plain flour
- ➤ ¾ cup oats

Tools that you will need:

- ➤ Mixing bowl
- ➤ Scales
- ➤ Cup measurers
- ➤ Baking Tray
- ➤ Baking liner
- ➤ Wooden Spoon
- ➤ Cooling Rack

What you need to do:

- ➤ First turn your oven on to 175 degrees centigrade (350 degrees Fahrenheit).

- ➤ Then get your mixing bowl and add your oats and add in the butter and sugar and mix them all together with your wooden spoon.

- ➤ Slowly add in your golden syrup and mix together. Then slowly add in the flour and mix together until it comes together to form a sort of dough. Then take balls of the dough and squash them down into a round shape on the baking tray. Then put the tray of biscuits into the oven to cook for 10 minutes or until they are golden.

HOMEMADE OREOS
– best ever says my Mum and she doesn't like Oreos!

Ingredients:

- 225g butter
- 200g Caster sugar
- 2 teaspoons table salt
- 2 large eggs
- 250g Plain Flour
- 150g cocoa powder
- ½ teaspoon baking soda

For filling:

- 115g butter
- 240g icing sugar
- 1 teaspoon vanilla essence

Tools that you will need:

- 3 Mixing Bowls
- Scales
- Electric Mixer

- Sieve
- Wooden spoon
- Cling Film
- Rolling Pin
- Rolling Mat
- Baking Parchment
- Cookie Cutter
- Baking Tray
- Baking Liner
- Cooling Rack

What you should do:

- First grab one of your mixing bowls and put in your butter, caster sugar and salt and mix with the electric mixer until it is all light and fluffy. Then add in the eggs and mix in with the electric mixer.

- Then in your second bowl mix together your sieved flour, cocoa powder and baking soda. Then pour this mix into your first bowl and stir with your wooden spoon until it is all mixed together. You should then have a dough like mixture. Push it together and wrap it in cling film and put it in the fridge for about an hour.

- Turn your over into 160 degrees centigrade (325 degrees Fahrenheit)

- Take your dough out of the fridge. Now you need to roll it out. As it is quite big, only take half out at a time and roll it between two bits of baking parchment until it is about 1/2cm thick. Cut the dough into rounds using a small cookie cutter and place on the lined baking tray.

Leave space between the cookies on the tray as they spread when they are cooked! Once you have done the first half of the dough you can take the other half out of the fridge and do the same again.

➢ The cookies need to be in the oven for about 15mins and then they can be put on the cooling rack to cool while you make the filling.

➢ Get your 3rd mixing bowl and mix together the butter, icing sugar and vanilla essence using the electric mixer. The cookies must be completely cool before you put the fulling in otherwise it all melts!

➢ Put the filling between two cookies and you have the best Oreos ever says my Mummy – and she doesn't even like Oreos!

PANCAKES
– I love pancakes any time of day!

Ingredients:

- ➤ 3 eggs
- ➤ 1 cup of milk
- ➤ 2 tablespoons plain flour
- ➤ Butter

Tools that you will need

- ➤ Mixing bowl
- ➤ Tablespoon measurer
- ➤ Frying pan
- ➤ Cup measure
- ➤ Whisk
- ➤ Ladle
- ➤ Pancake flipper

What you need to do:

- ➤ First you get your mixing bowl and you put your milk and eggs in and mix them together with the whisk. Then slowly add in your flour and whisk in.

- ➢ Put your frying pan on a medium heat and melt a little butter in the pan. Use your ladle to spoon some mixture into the frying pan and start cooking the pancake. You can use the pancake flipper to turn the pancake over and cook the other side of the pancake.
- ➢ Then you'll have the best pancakes ever!!
- ➢ TIP: you can add fruit, lemon, sugar or maple syrup

RAINBOW CAKE
– needs a lot of pans and colouring but it is so pretty!

Ingredients:

- ➢ 250g Butter
- ➢ 450g Plain Flour
- ➢ 300g golden caster sugar or normal if you don't have golden
- ➢ 6 medium eggs
- ➢ 2 teaspoon baking powder
- ➢ 2 teaspoon vanilla extract
- ➢ Food colouring – red, orange yellow, green, blue and purple

For butter icing:

- ➢ 200g Butter
- ➢ 250g Icing Sugar
- ➢ 1 teaspoon water

Tools you will need:

- ➢ Electric mixer
- ➢ Sandwich tins – 6 if possible, otherwise you will need to

keep washing and using the same ones

- ➤ Baking Parchment
- ➤ Large Bowl
- ➤ 6 small bowls
- ➤ 6 dessert spoons
- ➤ Cooling racks
- ➤ Scales
- ➤ Skewer
- ➤ Wooden spoon
- ➤ Spatula
- ➤ Large plate or cake board

What you need to do:

- ➤ Turn your oven on to 180 degrees centigrade (360 degrees Fahrenheit). Grease and line your sandwich tins.
- ➤ Then take your large mixing bowl and put in your butter and sugar and mix with your electric mixer. Then add the eggs two at a time and mix with the electric mixer. Stir in the vanilla extract with your wooden spoon. Then mix in the flour and baking powder with your wooden spoon.
- ➤ Then separate this mixture into the 6 small bowls. Add two or three drops of the different food colourings into each bowl and mix each one with a different spoon. Then put each coloured mixture into a separate sandwich tin.
- ➤ Then put in the oven for 10-15 minutes until when you put a skewer in, it comes out clean. Let the cakes cool on a cooling rack.
- ➤ Then put the purple cake at the bottom, cover with butter

icing using your spatula, then the blue cake and then more icing, then the green cake and more butter icing and then the yellow cake and another layer of icing. Then the orange cake with more butter icing and the red cake on top. Then cover the whole cake with a thin layer of butter icing.

TIP: Add rainbow sprinkles as well!

RED VELVET CUPCAKES

Ingredients:

- 150g Plain Flour
- 1 tablespoon cocoa powder
- 1 teaspoon bicarbonate of soda
- 50 g soft butter
- 150g caster sugar
- 1 large egg – beaten
- 1 teaspoon vanilla extract
- 100ml buttermilk or you can use regular milk
- 50ml vegetable oil like sunflower oil
- 1 tablespoon of red gel food colouring
- Icing: see butter icing recipe

Tools you will need:

- Cupcake tin
- Cupcake cases
- Sieve
- Scales
- Teaspoon measurer
- Tablespoon measure
- Measuring jug

- ➢ 2 Medium mixing bowls
- ➢ Wooden spoon
- ➢ Electric mixer or hand whisk
- ➢ Metal teaspoons
- ➢ Skewer
- ➢ Cooling rack

What you will need to do:

- ➢ Line the cupcake tin with cases. Turn the oven to 180 degrees centigrade (355 degrees Fahrenheit).
- ➢ Sieve the flour, cocoa powder and bicarbonate of soda into the mixing bowl and mix with your wooden spoon. Then take your second bowl and using your electric mixer or whisk beat together the butter and sugar until light and fluffy. Then beat in the egg, vanilla essence, milk and oil into this mixture until they are all combined.
- ➢ Gradually mix the wet ingredients into the dry ingredients using your wooden spoon. Once they are mixed together, mix in the red gel food colouring with a metal spoon. Put the mixture into your cupcake cases using your teaspoons. Bake for 15 mins until your skewer comes out clean. Put your cupcakes to cool on the rack

TIP: Add butter icing, see page 64, to the top of the cupcakes when cool

SHORTCAKE
- yummy!

Ingredients:

- ➤ 225g Plain flour
- ➤ 1 teaspoon baking powder
- ➤ 3 eggs
- ➤ 1 pinch of cream of tartar
- ➤ 300g caster sugar
- ➤ 110g soft butter
- ➤ 1 teaspoon vanilla extract
- ➤ 115 ml milk

Tools that you will need:

- ➤ 1 teaspoon measurer
- ➤ Scales
- ➤ Bowl
- ➤ Wooden spoon
- ➤ Round baking tin

What you will need to do:

- ➤ First you turn the oven to 175 degrees centigrade (350 degrees Fahrenheit).

➤ Then you get your bowl and add your flour and your baking powder and your cream of tartar and then you mix these together with your wooden spoon. Then you add your eggs in one at a time and mix again. Then you start adding in your sugar and the soft butter. Then you mix again. Next you add in your vanilla extract and the milk and mix together again.

➤ Then you put your mixture in your greased or lined baking tin and push down with the back of the spoon and put it in the oven for 35 minutes. Then you take it out and let it cool.

TIP: you can add icing or topping if you want to make it more exciting!

SMOOTHIE ICE LOLLIES
– easy if you have a blender!

Ingredients:

- ➢ 10 strawberries
- ➢ 2 ½ bananas
- ➢ ¼ tub of yoghurt

Tools that you need:

- ➢ Cutting board
- ➢ Knife
- ➢ Blender/smoothie maker
- ➢ Baking Tray or Ice Cube Tray

What you need to do:

- ➢ First you chop your strawberries and bananas on your chopping board. Then you add them to your smoothie maker and blender with the yoghurt and blend. Pour the mixture into the ice cube tray with ice lolly sticks in the middle or put it on a baking tray and place in the freezer and freeze

VANILLA CUPCAKES
– nice and simple!

Ingredients:

- ➤ 200g Plain Flour
- ➤ 1 teaspoon baking powder
- ➤ 1 teaspoon bicarbonate of soda
- ➤ 200g butter
- ➤ 200g caster sugar
- ➤ 5 eggs
- ➤ 3 teaspoons vanilla extract

Tools you will need:

- ➤ 2 mixing bowls
- ➤ 1 teaspoon measurer
- ➤ Scales
- ➤ Wooden spoon
- ➤ Cupcake Tray
- ➤ Cupcake cases
- ➤ Electric Mixer
- ➤ Metal spoons
- ➤ Cooling rack

What you will need to do:

> ➢ First you need to turn the oven on to 180 degrees centigrade (350 degrees Fahrenheit) and put cupcake cases in your cupcake tray.

> ➢ Then you grab your first bowl and add your flour and then you add your baking powder and your bicarbonate of soda and mix it all together with your wooden spoon.

> ➢ Then you get your second bowl and add your butter and sugar and mix it together with your electric mixer and then slowly add your eggs one at a time and mix. Then once you've mixed that all up you add your vanilla extract. Then grab your first bowl with the flour mixture and slowly stir this in using your wooden spoon again.

> ➢ Then using your metal spoons, spoon the cupcake mixture into your cupcake cases and put into the oven for 10-15 mins or until lightly brown and when you take them out you will have the best cupcakes ever!

TIP: You can ice these cupcakes with butter or glace icing. And even put different sprinkles of decorations on them!

ICING RECIPES

Butter Icing:

➢ You need butter, icing sugar and a small amount of water. You can also add vanilla extract or cocoa powder if you want a different flavour.

➢ Mix the ingredients with an electric mixer until fluffy. Or you can mix with a whisk or spoon if the butter is soft.

Glace Icing:

➢ Use a little bit of water and icing sugar and mix together with a metal spoon in a small bowl until a little runny.

www.laralovesbaking.com

Printed in Poland
by Amazon Fulfillment
Poland Sp. z o.o., Wrocław

64003028R00056